Reflections in the Baubles

An Advent to Epiphany course

Helen Warwick

kevin mayhew

kevin mayhew

First published in Great Britain in 2012 by Kevin Mayhew Ltd
Buxhall, Stowmarket, Suffolk IP14 3BW
Tel: +44 (0) 1449 737978 Fax: +44 (0) 1449 737834
E-mail: info@kevinmayhewltd.com

www.kevinmayhew.com

ISBN 978 1 84867 5278
Catalogue No. 1501359

Cover design by Rob Mortonson
© Images used under licence from Shutterstock Inc.
Edited by Lawrence Osborn
Typeset by Richard Weaver

Printed and bound in Great Britain

For Betty

With many thanks to Anne and her housegroup WOW
(Women on the Way).

Thank you to my Worth housegroup.

About the author

Helen Warwick is a spiritual director and writer. She is a trained occupational therapist and has done various counselling courses, including person-centred art therapy. She works with people individually and runs courses and retreats. Her passion is to help others with their journey through life using a creative approach. Helen's other books published by Kevin Mayhew are: *Creating Gardens in the Desert* (1501092) and *Finding Your Inner Treasure* (1501247).

Contents

Introduction

Advent to Epiphany is ideally a period in the year when one takes time to reflect on the coming of Jesus and what his presence means in our world. The reality of this period is that it can be a difficult time for many people. Alongside the joy, candlelight, social events and holy space, there can be concerns that threaten to overwhelm. Anxiety and stress may dominate these weeks, rather than the peace that Jesus offers. Many issues are highlighted in the bid to make Christmas Day a successful celebration. Shops start enticing buyers months earlier; there is an expectation to send cards and buy presents. Family relationships have to be negotiated, people cared for and painful memories coped with. Coming in the depths of winter in Britain can add to the darkness some experience. By the time you have hung the baubles onto the Christmas tree they may be reflecting a room full of chaos rather than the light of Jesus. This course will be addressing some of the concerns that come about during this period and how we are affected by them. It will be looking at what Jesus offers in the tensions, busyness and suffering of everyday life.

Up until Christmas 2010 my Advent period and Christmas celebrations had been fairly predictable. My circumstances may have varied but there was the usual busyness with cards and presents as well as acknowledging the special time of year. Christmas Day was always spent with family alongside church, food, presents, fun and laughter. Christmas 2010 proved to be very different. Our son was spending a year in an American university and we were going to visit him for a unique family holiday, spending Christmas Day in New York. God had other plans. I came down with a bad virus a couple of weeks before we were due to leave and my body decided it wasn't going to get better in a hurry. So the big decision had to be made that I would stay at home while the rest of the family went and did America. A few days before Christmas I had no idea what I would do on Christmas Day but, being in a fragile state, I just trusted in God's plans. I was completely surprised and encouraged by how my Christmas panned out. A few days before the twenty-fifth I visited an elderly lady, Betty, who was interested in one of my books. I didn't know her very well but we had a pleasant chat and as I was leaving she happened to mention that she had no one to share her Christmas dinner. She always organised a dinner to share with others who would like some company on Christmas Day. However, the people she had asked all had other plans. I hesitated a moment – I knew I had family offers of Christmas celebrations, but I was feeling very weary and could not cope with the thought of noisy gatherings. Having seen her peaceful home, with the jigsaw out on the table and the knitting by the settee, I mentioned my situation and to my great surprise it was agreed that we would spend some time together on that special day. So I had the most peaceful Christmas that I have ever had. I went to her small church in the morning. We then went back to Betty's house where she offered me her bed to rest while she prepared the dinner. There were no presents, just peace and fellowship. Betty was able to bring Jesus alive, not only with her stories, but having shared some of my story, she felt led to wash my feet in a very sacred act after our lunch. Even though there were other kind people who had offered me hospitality, this was a hospitality that met so many needs in me and provided such a healing space.

It is so easy to get bogged down with the expectations of others and the materialistic pressures of this season. Experiencing Jesus in action, having him at the centre of that day brought home to me the importance of what Christmas is about and how that can minister and heal. It reminded me of the true reason of Christmas: to connect to Jesus as the human representation of God. Paul mentions this in his second letter to the Corinthians 'For God, who said, "Let light shine out of darkness," made his light shine in our hearts to give us the light of the knowledge of the glory of God in the face of Christ' (2 Corinthians 4:6). It is Jesus who enlightens us with the knowledge of God. It is through him that we are able to connect to God. Developing our relationship with Jesus will be the focus of this course.

This course helps to highlight a period in the calendar that is worth reflecting upon; not only on God's glory displayed in Christ, but also on what the issues we experience reveal about ourselves. Problems that take us out of our comfort zone, although uncomfortable, can uncover areas within us that are worth the reflection. This course will allow some sacred space to explore what affects us and enable tools to find God in various concerns that will be useful for any time of year.

About the course

Each week starts with an introduction that provides reflection and preparation for the following session. The first week looks at observing with Jesus' perspective. The next four weeks each highlight issues that the period of Advent can often accentuate. These include finding space in the busyness, coping with temptations and needs, tackling the expectations of others and coping with suffering. Each of these sessions has a character that highlights these aspects. Within each week there is opportunity to reflect on your own circumstances and issues and to look at the person God is moulding you to be. The course finishes with connecting to the joy and celebration that Jesus offers.

Many of the activities offered use a creative approach. I have had a lot of experience introducing creative activities to help people understand themselves better and their relationship with God. They often uncover a perspective that is difficult to reach through logical thinking. It is like looking at a pond. You cannot see the reflection that is on the water at the same time as looking at what is in the pond. You have to adjust your eyes to look at one or the other perspective. We often only see the reflection of ourselves through others or what we think about ourselves. Creative ways tend to search in the pond, rather than the reflection on the water, and unveil what is there. This can be profound and have all sorts of reactions. Both treasures and debris might be revealed: so reactions such as tears, puzzlement and unease may be experienced as well as enlightenment, joy and a sense of wonder. Bringing Jesus' perspective into the creative experience will add a dimension that helps to cope with what your pond reveals.

Most people I introduce to creative activities say that they are not creative *at all.* I always reassure them as I take them through step by step and they see for themselves how power-ful these activities can be. I introduced one lady to using her imagination and to meeting Jesus in her imagination. This is what she said: 'Visualisation has taken me on a journey that I did not think I was capable of. It took me out of my comfort zone into territory which enabled me to realise two things. Firstly, for many years I thought I was searching for Jesus and he was not answering my call, but I found he was there all the time waiting for me to come and meet me. Secondly, through this journey I have been brought to a place of peace and serenity, a harbour that I can access, wherever I am, whenever I want.'

There is a creative activity for each session in the book. They are set out clearly, in a way where the group or indi-vidual can easily organise themselves. There are no right and wrongs with these activities. If they are interpreted differently then that itself is a sign of creativity. I am always delighted when people tell me they did not do what I suggested as they are using their own creativity and what is right for them. There will be no need for analysis of the activity, as people will understand what God leads them to understand. If there is no understanding of what has come up then it might be revealed in the coming days or it may not be the right time for understanding. Each individual will be different and what is important is what comes up for them and not what others input to their experience. God needs to be relied upon as the best leader and counsellor for what is revealed from the pond and to provide what is needed when things are revealed. That is not to say that others cannot be supportive and be good listeners – these activities may bring a deeper understanding to groups. We are all made creative beings by a creative God and I would encourage you to try out activities and see where they lead you and your group.

The course is written for group work, but can be worked through by individuals, although finding a friend to work with may allow more support and interest. It will be helpful if each member doing the course has a copy of the book as it enriches the sessions if people have read the introduction first and have had time to reflect and prepare.

Note for leaders

For each session I have included a lot of material. Do be flexible with timings. If the 'short discussion' is proving valuable then perhaps leave it a little longer. The same goes for the creative activity where people might want to share for longer, although many may find their experience too personal to share. I suggest that people share in pairs for some of the meeting; you decide whether some of this might be beneficial as a group.

I also include a further activity at the end of each week. This is there for various reasons: you could swap it for the activity suggested if you prefer, or people could use it as a follow-on after the session. You could also split each session into two separate weeks, meaning that you have an activity for each one and have more time to explore the issue set out. Take the course at a pace that is right for your group, don't try to rush it and squeeze it into six weeks if it would be advantageous to take longer.

As the leader, do not assume any great responsibility, only to follow what I have set out step by step. However, you do need to be aware of the impact that some of the activities and issues may bring up. These sessions will not be pain-free as they will be enabling people to look a bit deeper into themselves and their relationship with God. You will need to provide a caring environment where people listen to each other and where they are not judged or criticised. Encourage the group to reflect on each session with God. You could also encourage individuals to get the support they need if issues do stir up a lot in their pond, for instance, the support of a friend, or there are always good counsellors and spiritual directors in each community. Do not shoulder responsibilities on yourself that are unnecessary.

I include the Bible passages in this book, but you may like to have some more translations available for the sessions to provide a wider perspective on the passages.

I hope it will be an enriching time to enable people to draw closer to Jesus.

Week 1

Opening the blinds

Introduction

Advent can be a time of joy and celebration; a time of reviewing our closeness to God and taking opportunity for more space with him. It can also be a time when life gets busy with extra events planned and more to organise. In this first week there is opportunity to reflect on what concerns you might experience through this time and how you have to compromise. There will be a focus on opening our spiritual vision to try and see life through Jesus' perspective.

To help with the observations over the whole Advent period, this week will be focusing on opening our spiritual vision or our inner eye. Eyes are mentioned many times in the Bible, from the opening of the eyes of Adam and Eve in Genesis 3:5-7 to the description of the eyes of Christ in John's revelation (Revelation 19:12 for example). Many biblical references to eyes include a broader description than just physical sight. They refer to mental and spiritual abilities, the capacity to see God's perspective clearly. When Adam and Eve's eyes were opened they revealed an intimate knowledge of good and evil. When referring to the inner eye I am highlighting a connection to God and seeing his perspective.

There are many passages in the Bible where Jesus encourages people to open their understanding and insight. In Matthew 13:11-16 Jesus explains why he speaks in parables. He knew that people who had not opened their inner eyes would not understand the message, but for those who did open their eyes there was a chance of understanding with their hearts and for healing from Jesus. He said 'blessed are your eyes because they see, and your ears because they hear.

For I tell you the truth, many prophets and righteous men longed to see what you see but did not see it, and to hear what you hear and did not hear it' (Matthew 13:16, 17).

Prayer and Bible study are some ways to connect with the inner eye. Another method I find helpful for cultivating the inner eye is to use the imagination. The imagination is a fantastic tool; it can bring up images that help acknowledge our feelings, find memories to work through and produce images to calm our minds. It is something that we all have, so you need no materials and can tap into its resource any time of day or night. Some people may have difficulty using the imagination because it may have become rusty over the years; we all have an imagination and its activation can really help give another perspective to exploring our situation and relationship with God. I myself find using the imagination an invaluable tool, enhancing both prayer and Bible study, to gain a spiritual understanding of my circumstances and my relationship with God.

The way I am introducing the imagination in the following session is to use it to focus on Jesus and his perspective. Picturing Jesus in our minds can be difficult and some people prefer just to sense a presence that is with them. I have introduced similar exercises to many people who have really appreciated its value.

Each week of this course there is some encouragement to prepare for the session to come. This week it is to reflect on what your ideal Advent period would be like. You may have mixed feelings about Advent. It can be a really joyous time with more socials, family times, sitting by warm fires and connecting to God. It can also be a difficult time when life gets busier with all the traditions that have evolved with this period such as sending cards, buying presents, decorating trees and houses, and having social events. Coming in the winter time, the longer spells of darkness can exacerbate some of the problems around for people. Loneliness, suffering and painful memories can be other aspects to this Advent time.

Preparation

Imagine what you would really like in this Advent period and what you feel you need. It might not be a time that you have really thought about before, or it might be a period that you wish you could bypass every year. What would be your ultimate Christmas Day, the culmination of this period? Then compare this with the reality of your Advent. What are some of the issues that crop up for you? Where do you have to compromise and what feelings does that provoke?

Session 1: Opening the blinds

Equipment

Bible, pens and paper.

Quiet time

Start the meeting with some silence. Encourage people in the silence to open their eyes and then close their eyes. Just to notice being in the silence with eyes open and then eyes closed.

Opening prayer

Lord, as we gather to be with you, help us to connect to the true meaning of the Advent period and to gain your insight. Enable us to take your eye test so we can open up our eyes in wonder and belief. Amen.

Commentary

This week we are looking at the issues that can crop up around the Advent period. We will be thinking about the spiritual vision or inner eye that God offers us and using an activity that opens our inner eyes.

Short discussion

Discuss in pairs your ideal Advent period, the sort of things you would like to include and also avoid. What would your ideal Christmas Day look like? What compromises do you have to make over this time and what feelings does that bring up for you?

Bible reading

Read Matthew 6:22, 23. Ideally use different versions.

This is *The Message* version, where Jesus says:

> 'Your eyes are windows into your body. If you open your eyes wide in wonder and belief, your body fills up with light. If you pull the blinds on your windows, what a dark life you will have.'

This week we are looking at connecting to this spiritual eye, our inner eye. Spiritual vision is our capacity to see clearly what God wants for us and to see the world from his point of view. *The Message* refers to the eyes as windows into your body. Opening the inner eye gives insight and understanding into God's way of doing things, it enlightens us. If we don't connect to this spiritual vision it is like having the blinds continually pulled down over our eyes and we live a dark life.

Short discussion

How do our physical eyes differ from the spiritual eye that Jesus talks about in this verse? What are people's experience of this connection to insight and understanding?

Jesus came to earth as a baby, experiencing the world through his senses. I can imagine him taking in the scenes with keen observation, babies being especially entranced by people's faces. In Jesus' ministry he noticed different aspects about people; he had that special insight. He also faced each issue as he came to it. He stayed connected to God, and one way he did this was to reflect on situations and pray. We read that one place for his prayer was the mountainside. This is a good position for reflection but also observation – from up high you are not only in a quiet place but a good vantage point for overseeing. In Mark 6:45-48 we read that Jesus had gone up to the mountainside to pray after spending time teaching and feeding at least 5000 people. He had sent the disciples off in the boat so he could have some solitary time. Jesus was able to see the disciples struggling with the boat from that vantage point. He then went out to calm the storm and rescue them.

The following activity uses the imagination to connect to the inner eye by imagining sitting with Jesus. This is observing from a non-judgemental place, a place where there is a stillness, from a perspective that links to God.

The leader needs to reassure people not to worry if they cannot picture anything; they just need to sit quietly and see what happens. Also reassure people that if they lose track of what has been said, or do their own thing, then that is fine too. The meditation needs to be read out line by line, leaving long pauses (up to two minutes) between lines, especially towards the end, so people have time to use their imagination to the full. It should take about 15 minutes.

Activity

Sit comfortably with both feet flat on the floor. Spend a few moments just focusing on your breath.

Try to let go of any thoughts – let them pass over like clouds.

Now imagine you are on a mountainside. Just imagine this scene.

Try to feel the terrain and the textures around you.

You sit down on this mountainside. You look out at the view before you. It might not be clear at first, just see what emerges.

You realise that sitting next to you is Jesus. You might be able to see him in human form, or just feel his presence.

Talk to Jesus about any concerns. Listen to his answer.

Note any changes that might be happening in the scene.

Acknowledge what has gone on for you and note your feelings.

Then slowly bring yourself back into the room.

Give everyone a few minutes to note down anything they would like to.

Split into pairs for some time of sharing, making it clear that no one *has* to share, as there might be sensitive issues. Sometimes just asking how that activity was for people, for example, how difficult it was to use the imagination can be helpful.

This activity involved linking to Jesus in the imagination and trying to see and hear through his perspective. This can be a good way to reflect on problems and issues with Jesus. Throughout Advent this might be a tool you may like to use to observe issues that are coming up for you. From that mountainside you could oversee these issues and talk through them with Jesus.

Summary

Perhaps there could be a regular time set aside to observe the day from the mountainside with Jesus. The more the blinds are opened the more light is let in.

Prayer

Finish with a time of prayer, allowing people to reflect on this session.

Further activity

Matthew 7:3-5 talks about removing the plank in your own eye before taking the sawdust out of another's eye.

'Why do you look at the speck of sawdust in your brother's eye and pay no attention to the plank in your own eye? How can you say to your brother, "Let me take the speck out of your eye," when all the time there is a plank in your own eye? You hypocrite, first take the plank out of your own eye, and then you will see clearly to remove the speck from your brother's eye.'

It is easy for our inner eye to get clouded. Our planks are often made up of egocentric issues: self-serving desires and interests can block our vision if they are not connected to the vision that God has for our lives. There is often a discrepancy between what we think we want and what we need. Use your imagination to look at this plank in your own eye and talk with Jesus as to how best to remove it. How could this experience be used to help another with the sawdust in their eye?

Week 2

Is the grass really greener?

Introduction

There was a song that was popular with my children when they were small. It was by an American who called himself 'The Doughnut Man'. The words included the phrase 'Life without Jesus is like a doughnut, there's a hole in the middle of your soul'. Advent can be a time when the holes in our soul feel darker and deeper. We all have needs and sometimes it is hard for us to find fulfilment in our faith and let God meet our deepest needs.

This week we will be looking at our own circumstances and needs, noticing the times when we reach out for comforts to try to meet these holes within our souls. These holes could be connected to feelings of emptiness, inadequacy, shame, guilt, anxiety, anger, frustration and many other issues. In this week's session we meet Emma who struggles with feelings of loneliness and turns to food and drink for comfort. Following this we will be looking at what Jesus offers to help with our needs.

Doctor Larry Crabb, an American counsellor, notes that we often head for goals that are outside our reach. 'Whenever a person sets out to achieve a goal which responsible effort does not guarantee, he experiences what I call Basic Anxiety.'[1] Anxiety can happen when we crave what is outside the limits of our abilities – often leading us to try to satisfy ourselves in ways which we feel are not right. Larry Crabb goes on to say that we often misplace our dependency – we depend on everything *but* God. Jesus comes to offer a renewing of our minds so that we can work on what we believe we must have, in order to feel truly worthwhile.

The activity in the session gives an insight into what we have now. This will be a creative way of using colour. Many people who are faced with felt-tips and paper are initially fearful of drawing. Thoughts of being able to draw well or produce something that looks good block the creative process. For any type of creative imagining it is important to stress that the end result does not have to look perfect; it is more about noting what happens when you put colour to paper and what you are reminded of in the end result. I have used creative art with many people who always say they are not creative at all, and yet they can see that the end result tells them more about themselves than if they had tried to describe their circumstances in words. It can be a powerful medium.

Last week explored the inner eye, being the observer with Jesus on the mountainside. This is a good vantage point to oversee episodes in your life. This week this position can be used to be an observer of yourself and how you cope with your needs. The times when you feel needy – what do you do? What do you reach out for to try to fill that hole?

Preparation

Observe the times this week when you reach out for something to fill a need. Note what you are feeling at the time. Just observe what you do to help yourself.

Session 2: Is the grass really greener?

Equipment

Bible, paper plates (one for each person), felt-tips, coloured pencils.

Quiet time

Sit quietly in God's presence. Notice any tensions you are

holding in your body. Breathe into each of these areas and try to release the tension as you sit in the silence.

Opening prayer

Lord, we pray you will be in our midst as we think about our circumstances. You are the One who says 'You may ask me for anything in my name, and I will do it.'[2] We pray that we can be led by you now and look to you for guidance and renewal. Amen.

Commentary

In this session we are looking at how we cope with our different needs and how we can look more to Jesus to help meet our needs.

This is Emma's situation:

> These are my thoughts on Advent. All the temptation around is difficult for me. I like my food and drink. Around Christmas time with all the extra social events and mince pies at every occasion I find it difficult to not just stuff myself all the time. And alcohol – I know it is not good for me but I love that warm cosy feeling it gives me. I am not very happy in my relationship with my partner at the moment. So I know I am using food and drink for comfort. My frustration and longing I find difficult to cope with, so every time I get upset I head to the kitchen. I don't like myself when I do this but this is how I cope at the moment. It is worse around this period, especially as there is someone at church who is trying to get friendly with me. I really don't want to muddle up my life even more, but the darker nights, the candle light, the loneliness I am feeling keep pulling me towards what I know will confuse the issues more. I feel a deep need for more connection with God but he doesn't seem to be there.

Short discussion

In pairs discuss some of the ways in which you reach out to meet your needs, for example when you are angry, lonely or confused. How do you connect to God at these times? What would you suggest for Emma?

At this Advent time we think of Jesus being born as a baby. His coming was in difficult conditions. Mary and Joseph must have wanted something very different for the birth. Yet God knew that they had all they needed. As that baby, Jesus had all he needed to thrive, and Mary and Joseph had all they needed to be the father and mother that were right for Jesus.

Adam and Eve started off in the Garden of Eden. God gave them all they needed in this idyllic environment. Problems came for them when they started looking outside of their needs. They wanted more than they had been given, a goal outside God's agenda. They were tempted by the offer of achieving this in their own way, rather than the way God ordained.

The following activity helps to look at our circumstances. This will be in the form of our own garden – a fictitious garden. Using a creative way of exploring can expand and enlighten us about our circumstances. The best way to get into this activity is not to think about it, just go for it!

Activity

Give out paper plates and colouring materials.

On your paper plate use the colours to represent a garden. This is going to be a garden of your circumstances, what is in your life at this moment in time. Don't try to draw perfect images. Use colours to squiggle and doodle – just as self-expression. Just pick up a colour that attracts you and make some marks on the plate. Either side of the plate can be used – the shiny or the matt side. Note the boundary of the plate. You might find you have neat areas, messy areas, flowers, weeds, compost, water and spaces. Just see what happens as you connect to the colours. Don't worry if the end result just looks like splodges – that is fine.

You have 10 minutes for this activity and will not need to show the end result to anyone if you don't want to.

Leave some time for individual reflection.

After this activity, split into pairs to share how that activity was for you. Stress that people do not have to share anything personal.

The gardens may have highlighted difficult areas or areas that look like they need sorting, but it is within this garden that God will be able to develop you into the person he has made you to be. The paper plate has a boundary. Looking at something outside this boundary – either having goals that are unattainable or looking at your neighbour's greener grass for instance, can lead to difficulties in life. God is described as the gardener by Jesus; he is the God of transformation. We can only have Jesus transform us if we are willing for him to come and do some gardening, rather than looking outside the boundaries of our garden for some other way to meet our needs.

Emma found that her garden had an area of thick brambles and also a deep pool. She did not understand what everything meant but felt like she should be spending more time in this garden to sort out the brambles and tidy and weed. She knew that she expected a lot from her partner, wanting understanding and more of a feeling of security. Letting the garden highlight things for her over a few days made her want to see what happened to areas of the garden when she talked to God about what was going on for her.

Jesus was able to offer people a way to fill the holes in their souls and transform their gardens. We look next to a passage in the Bible early on in Jesus' ministry where he starts to highlight this way.

Bible reading

Read from John 1:35-39

> The next day John was there again with two of his disciples. When he saw Jesus passing by, he said, 'Look, the Lamb of God!' When the two disciples heard him say this, they followed

Jesus. Turning around, Jesus saw them following and asked, 'What do you want?' They said, 'Rabbi' (which means 'Teacher'), 'where are you staying?' 'Come,' he replied, 'and you will see.' So they went and saw where he was staying, and they spent that day with him. It was about four in the afternoon.

This is a short passage showing how two disciples of John the Baptist, probably Andrew and John, started to follow Jesus. Jesus realised he was being followed, turned to face the disciples and asked them what they wanted. I wonder what your reaction to Jesus would have been if he asked you what you wanted? I think I might have replied that I want some answers to some very tricky questions that are around for me at present. Andrew and John wanted to know practicalities – where Jesus was staying. Jesus seems keen to show them as they spend the rest of the day with him.

Later on, when Jesus talks to the disciples about an image of the vine, he goes on to say: 'Live in me. Make your home in me just as I do in you. In the same way that a branch can't bear grapes by itself but only by being joined to the vine, you can't bear fruit unless you are joined with me' (John 15:4 *The Message*).

We find out that Jesus not only invites us to his home but he states that he *is* the home. He encourages us to make our home in him so that he can make his home in us. Henri Nouwen, a Dutch priest, continues with this thought:

> Jesus, in whom the fullness of God dwells, has become our home. By making his home in us he allows us to make our home in him. By entering into the intimacy of our innermost self he offers us the opportunity to enter into his own intimacy with God. By choosing us as his preferred dwelling place he invites us to choose him as our preferred dwelling place. This is the mystery of the incarnation.[3]

Short discussion

Jesus asked the disciples 'What do you want?' What would be your answer? The disciples wanted to know where Jesus was staying. How do you imagine Jesus' home and circumstances? What would that be like if you had the dwelling of Jesus within you? How could you use this facility within you to help you with your needs?

Summary

We have tried a creative way of looking at our own circumstances as a garden. We look at what Jesus offers to help us with our needs as he dwells within us. What difference would this make if we give him our garden to cultivate?

Prayer

Take some time to reflect on this session. People might like to pray with their gardens. They could imagine Jesus coming into the garden and notice what might happen and whether anything changes.

Further activity

Take the John 1:35-39 verses and use your imagination to picture yourself as a disciple. Listen to what Jesus says to you and how he leads you to where he is staying. The disciples spent the rest of the day with Jesus. Imagine what you might do if you spent a few hours with Jesus.

1. Larry Crabb, *Effective Biblical Counselling* (Marshall Pickering), p. 134.
2. This Bible passage is from John 14:14.
3. Henri Nouwen, *Jesus: A Gospel* (Orbis Books), p. 35.

Week 3

Holding on to who I am

Introduction

We were all made as unique individuals at birth. This uniqueness can sometimes be affected by the pressure of what the world and other people are expecting of us, as well as our own expectations of what we think we should be achieving. These pressures can affect us all year round but are sometimes exacerbated at Christmas time, swayed by the many dictates of Advent and Christmas. This week we look at our uniqueness and how, as chosen individuals, we can stick to what is right for us with God. Paul's teaching to the Colossians will be assisting with this task.

In Week 1 there was an exploration of your ideal Advent period and what this period is really like for you. Some of the expectations of this time include writing and sending Christmas cards, buying and giving presents, putting up decorations, joining in social occasions, singing carols and thinking of those less privileged than ourselves. Where these few examples may be manageable and enjoyable to some, others may find they are pressured by the expectations of the traditions around at Christmas. I'm sure you can think of other areas where you do things because you feel you have to, where you do what is expected, rather than what you feel is right between you and God. In the session this week, we meet David with his thoughts.

Our reputations seem important to hold on to. I have a lovely aunt who has a very close walk with God. She tells others that she lost her reputation many years ago and that she loves the freedom it gives her! Jesus did not worry about what people thought of him. He did not allow this to change who he was and his connection to God. He told his friend to 'Get behind me Satan! You are a stumbling block to me' (Matthew 16:23); he upset the teachers of the law many times and caused utter chaos in the temple courts by up-turning the traders' tables (John 2:13-16). He walked away from people's needs when he wanted his own space with God and trusted in God to lead him to what was right to do or say. How easy do we find it to stick to what we feel God is leading us to do?

Karen Armstrong wrote about how important it is that we follow our own unique path:

> The great myths show that when you follow somebody else's path, you go astray. The hero has to set off by himself, leaving the old world and the old ways behind. He must venture into the darkness of the unknown, where there is no map and no clear route. He must fight his own monsters, not somebody else's, explore his own labyrinth, and endure his own ordeal before he can find what is missing in his life. Thus transfigured, he (or she) can bring something of value to the world that has been left behind. But if the knight finds himself riding along an already established track, he is simply following in somebody else's footsteps, and will not have an adventure. In the words of the Old French text of 'The Quest of the Holy Grail', if he wants to succeed, he must enter the forest 'at a point that he, himself, had chosen, where it was darkest and there was no path'. The waste land in the Grail legend is a place where people live in-authentic lives, blindly following the norms of their society and doing only what other people expect.[4]

Last week we noted in John 15:4 that Jesus invites us to make our home in him just as he does in us. By choosing us as his preferred dwelling place, he invites us to choose him as our preferred dwelling place. Jesus goes on to say to his disciples in John 15:16 'You did not choose me, but I chose you and appointed you.' God has chosen us to represent him in this life. If we have this royal appointment, how does that affect the way we go through Advent and are able to say 'yes' or 'no' to others? To find out the way that is right for us we first need to know more about who we really are.

Preparation

This week think about yourself as a unique, chosen individual. What are your gifts and passions? What makes you 'you'? Perhaps ask your close friends and family what gifts they see in you and get some feedback on yourself.

You may also like to read through Colossians chapter 2. We will be taking a few of these verses in the session; reading the whole chapter helps to put it all in context.

Session 3: Holding on to who I am

Equipment

Bible, A3 sheets of paper, magazines (enough for two each, the free ones are fine), scissors and glue sticks (enough for one between two), plastic bag or bin to tidy away scraps.

Quiet time

In the silence, imagine sitting at the feet of Jesus. You are sitting just as you are, coming just as yourself to be in his presence.

Opening prayer

Lord, we thank you for making each of us special. We thank you that you have chosen us to represent you. We pray for your guidance as we learn more of ourselves and how you lead us through these days. Amen.

Commentary

This week we are looking at our own uniqueness and how we can hold on to our uniqueness in a world with pressure for us to conform. The expectations of others and what we expect of ourselves can be a pressure that we are aware of all year round, but Advent can be a time when there is increased pressure to conform to traditions and family ties.

This is David's situation:

> Hi, I'm David and what I find difficult around Christmas are the expectations that abound. I hate drinking – socials are difficult for me. I also struggle with the giving thing. I'm not sure why presents are linked with the birth of Jesus, but somehow it is expected that all my friends and relatives have to be bought presents. Thanksgiving Day in America is a big celebration that includes family get-togethers and lovely food with no present giving. What a great way to celebrate! I would prefer to do some giving of my time. I like the idea of helping out at a soup kitchen or something like that. Last year I did a couple of sessions of carol singing along the local streets of our church, which I enjoyed. Anyway, I can feel that expectation on me to socialise, give presents, go to church, have a big grin on my face to show what a happy time I am having, and generally demonstrate that I love all the Christmas trimmings and baubles. I don't want to be a grump, but really when it gets to Christmas then I want to be able to relax, read a good book, have good food and rest. I feel I need to say 'no' more often to what crops up around this time (our work Christmas do is always appalling) and 'yes' to some giving to others. Perhaps in my quiet times with God I will ponder about how to do what I feel is more 'me' rather than doing things that I struggle with and feel others just want me to do. I want to try and find the strength to follow my own path through this time.

You may not relate to David's story, but we will all have areas of our lives where we feel pressure to do or say things that we know we aren't happy with, but there is a demand for us to do this. This demand might be from ourselves – to do what we think is right, or from other people. These areas pull us out of the shape we feel that we are made to be, they make us feel uncomfortable.

Short discussion

Discuss an example with your neighbour where you feel

e to conform or where there are expectations of
hat change what you feel is right for you to do. What
do these examples bring about?

heard a teacher say the following: 'If people were
1ore about who they are, they wouldn't have to be
t to do, it would come naturally.'⁵

Sometimes it is hard to look at ourselves in a positive way.
When we look in a mirror it is mainly the flaws that stand
out to us. In our thoughts there can be a critical voice beating
us down. A mirror does not show a true reflection of who
we are and it is good to find out what are our strong points.
God has given us all gifts and passions. It is good to explore
these so we can be clearer about our uniqueness and what
God may be asking of us. Knowing ourselves allows us to be
stronger and better able to stick to a path that is right for us.

The following activity will be using collage to gain some
insight into who you are – your gifts, passions and uniqueness. The activity is using magazines to find words and
pictures that tell us about ourselves. The idea is to flick
through the magazines, not getting bogged down in thinking
too much about what to look for, but just seeing what catches
your eye. Try not to get distracted with reading the articles!

Activity

Give out an A3 sheet for each person and explain that they
need to pick two magazines each. There should be scissors
and a glue stick to share between two people. The activity
needs to be timed into three sections of five minutes each.

1. Each person should flick through the magazines and
    find words that catch the eye. Find what speaks to you
    about yourself. Don't try to analyse why, just tear them
    out for now.
2. Go through the magazines again, this time finding
    pictures that catch your eye. Just tear out colours and
    images that attract you when you think about yourself.

3. The last five minutes is for you to cut and paste your snippets on to your A3 paper.

When you have finished look at what you have done and see what the A3 sheet says to you.

Have a tidy-away time.

Split into pairs for people to share how that was for them. Stress that people do not have to share anything personal.

Finding out more about yourself can help you make a stand for what is right for you. Our Bible study looks at the pressures and expectations on the Colossians and what Paul had to say to them about this.

Bible reading

Colossians 2:8-10 and 16-19. You may like to read two different versions.

> See to it that no one takes you captive through hollow and deceptive philosophy, which depends on human tradition and the basic principles of this world rather than on Christ. For in Christ all the fullness of the Deity lives in bodily form, and you have been given fullness in Christ, who is the head over every power and authority.
>
> Therefore do not let anyone judge you by what you eat or drink, or with regard to a religious festival, a New Moon celebration or a Sabbath day. These are a shadow of the things that were to come; the reality, however, is found in Christ. Do not let anyone who delights in false humility and the worship of angels disqualify you for the prize. Such a person goes into great detail about what he has seen, and his unspiritual mind puffs him up with idle notions. He has lost connection with the Head, from whom the whole body, supported and held together by its ligaments and sinews, grows as God causes it to grow.

Paul was talking to the Colossians, trying to counteract any false teaching that was opposed to Christ. Many false teachers were misleading the Colossians into ways that were unnecessary. For example, the Colossians believed they would progress to 'fullness' as Christians by keeping certain Jewish food taboos and rigidly observing their special days. There were pressures to conform to the right traditions.

The word 'fullness' is translated from the word *pleroma*, which refers to God in the completeness of his being, the entirety of all his attributes, his full divinity. It is this entirety that is in Christ that he revealed and communicated to others. Through Jesus we are offered that fullness: God in his entirety. Paul's criticism of the people who were going through the expected traditions and following the false teachings was that they were rejecting Christ as their Head. Paul was saying that Christ is the source of life and nourishment by which his body – the body of the Church – lives, and we need to be connected to this source of unity and become whole.

The more we are connected to Jesus, this source of unity, the stronger we are to withstand the expectations and persuasions of all that comes our way. It is making sure that the way we go through the Advent period – what we say 'yes' and 'no' to – is due to our connection to Jesus and what is the right way for us.

Our character David reflected with God on the Advent period and what he felt was right for him. He volunteered to help with the homeless for a couple of hours a week in the few weeks before Christmas and emailed his friends and family to ask for donations to this charity instead of giving him presents. He told them he would send no cards but would donate the money he would normally spend on these to this charity. He thought about Jesus' giving and imagined him as a carpenter perhaps making some gifts for others. He was reminded of his hobby of photography, which he really enjoyed, so he processed a few pictures to give to special friends. He felt a lot more connected to God through this Advent.

Short discussion

Using the Bible passage and your own examples reflect on how the pressures around you might affect the 'you' that has been explored in your collage.

If we have the completeness of God within us, having in Christ all that is required in life, how may that help us with the pressures and expectations of what is around? Is there anything we would like to do differently this Advent that connects to our special gifts and uniqueness in Christ?

Summary

How can your connection to Christ help you to keep your uniqueness in this world and resist pressures that take you away from the person you feel God has made you to be?

Prayer

Have some quiet reflecting on the session. People might like to reflect with their collage.

Further activity

'He has lost connection with the Head, from whom the whole body, supported and held together by its ligaments and sinews, grows as God causes it to grow' (Colossians 2:19).

Write down all the things that keep you connected to God as the Head. Try to brainstorm and write quickly so that things may appear that you had not thought about.

---

4. Karen Armstrong, *The Spiral Staircase* (Anchor Books), p. 301.
5. Rob Bell, *Velvet Elvis: Repainting the Christian Faith* (Zondervan), p. 144.

Week 4

Do you want to hear God's secret?

Introduction

Last week we were looking at our unique gifts and passions, and this week we will be thinking about opening our inner ears or our spiritual hearing to hear how God might be leading us on our unique paths.

Jesus came as a human to show us the way to God. We are the vessels, the chosen people that God chooses to use to enable his will in the world. Jesus says to his disciples in John 15:15, 'I no longer call you servants, because a servant does not know his master's business. Instead, I have called you friends, for everything that I learned from my Father I have made known to you.' Jesus shows us his Father and the way we can hear what God has to say to us.

Advent can be a busy time of the year. When life is hectic, especially if we are stressed, then it can be very difficult to hear God. We hear with our physical ears by detecting vibrations. These vibrations stimulate hair cells which send out electrical signals through nerve fibres to the brain. As we get older or are exposed to a lot of loud noise these hair cells die and do not get replaced and so our physical hearing deteriorates. To hear God we need some awareness of hearing with our spiritual ears, ears which are not affected with age. The inner ear tends to become more tuned into that divine voice the more we walk with God. These are ears that open the way to hear the voice of the Spirit, and the more we use them, the more open we are to God's promptings. In the book of Revelation John writes to seven churches in the first few chapters. Many times he records, 'He who has an ear let him hear what the Spirit says to the churches' (Revelation

2:7, 11, 17, 29; 3:6, 13, 22). Spiritual hearing is being open to what the Spirit is saying, not only for our personal journey, but also to help others on their journeys.

How well you can hear external sounds often depends on what is going on internally. When we are stressed we lose up to 80 per cent of our physical hearing. That is a lot we miss out on. Stress means that we have noise and chaos going on in our minds so we are unable to concentrate on the sounds that are around and what others are saying to us. To really listen to others and to God we need to have stilled our own internal agenda first.

One of the problems of hearing God at this Advent period can be finding time and space to be quiet with God. Perhaps this was part of God's plan after dropping the bombshell on Mary and Joseph about the forthcoming baby. They had to embark on a long journey to Bethlehem. Even though the journey would have been fraught with worries, it would have given them vital space to be with God and each other. It took them away from their everyday lives. Going along at walking pace would allow for reflection and ponderings. Maybe this was a time of refreshment for them with God, a time of strengthening for the weeks to come. In Matthew 6:6, Jesus teaches his disciples about prayer. He says, 'When you pray, go into your room and close the door and pray to your Father who is in secret; and your Father who sees in secret will reward you.' When we meet with God we hear what he wants to say to us for our unique journey. It is good to pray together to hear God, but we need to hear first what God has for us as a unique individual.

Many people ask me – how can I know that this is God speaking to me? How do I know I haven't just made something up? Well my thoughts are that we have God's Spirit within us, so I believe that whatever thoughts I have around, they are all connected to this Spirit of God. I know that God knows my every thought, action and response, so all my thoughts are connected to him. Regina Coupar writes

It is sad that we are so removed from the inner workings of our own soul that we often do not recognise the voice of divinity that is naturally within us. When such doubts arise, it is helpful to remember that the objective of our soul is love. If we are being led in the direction of love (of God *and* of others) we can know with confidence that it is our soul that beckons. As we peel away the layers of ego that separate us from our soul, we will free ourselves from the paralysing fear that prevents us from cultivating our intuition. We will make mistakes as we go along, but that is part of any learning process.[6]

Preparation

This week reflect on how you listen to God and how he communicates with you. Do you communicate with God? How can you tell you have a connection with God? Observe any internal chatter that you might have and how it affects your ability to listen to others and to God.

Note on the activity

The activity this week focuses on our listening. During the activity, the group will listen to three different kinds of sound. The range could include the following – the spoken word, music (any type), nature sounds (e.g. bird song or whale song). These can be played on a radio, CD player, computer or other portable media player. I have used a CD of bird song and music and then switched on a radio news channel for a few minutes in the activity. It does not matter what the words are; the exercise is about the ways we listen. The YouTube website is a good resource for nature sounds if you have no CD.

Session 4: Do you want to hear God's secret?

Equipment

Bible, any technical equipment that will help you play short excerpts of pieces to listen to (e.g. radio, CD player, computer, portable media player – see activity), paper and pens.

Quiet time

Sit quietly and just note what you can hear inside and outside the room. Really listen to all the depths of sound as well as the silence.

Opening prayer

Lord, we thank you for the blessing of our senses, especially our hearing. We pray that you open our inner ears tonight so we can learn more of you. Help us to expand our ways to connect to you. Amen.

Commentary

This week we are looking at how we can open our spiritual hearing to improve our relationship with God. Jesus told a lot of parables in his ministry. A parable is a story with a meaning. When the disciples asked Jesus why he spoke in parables, he replied, 'The knowledge of the secrets of the kingdom of heaven has been given to you' (Matthew 13:11). We are able to hear from God what the secrets of his kingdom are, what he wants for each of us and for his world as a whole. Connecting to God means that we hear God's secret messages that are for our ears and meet our own particular needs. Speaking in a hidden way, like finding the meaning in the parable for example, also means that we have to make an effort to hear what God has for us. God does not spell everything out to us clearly, because it is in the searching and uncovering that we experience all that God has in mind for us.

This is Stephen's situation:

Hi. My name is Stephen. What I struggle with most in the period leading up to Christmas is the increasing busyness. There seem to be more socials, which I am not really keen on, and a general lack of peace and quiet. I am a peaceful man who likes his space. I like to have time reflecting with just me and God. What with work commitments and general family organising and socials, I find I can go through the whole of Advent without much reflection. When I am busier, when I do come to God, I find it harder to connect to him as there is more going on in my mind. As I try and meditate I find my mind just wanders and busies itself with trying to sort out issues, such as what to get my mother for a Christmas present. I will try and get more discipline this year, as that is what I think I need. Just make myself sit quietly for a period each day, with my Bible and try and let go of any overwhelming thoughts.

Short discussion

In pairs, discuss how you connect to God. What are the difficulties you find in listening to God? How do you feel that he communicates with you? Is finding time and space a problem for you?

Opening up the inner or spiritual ear involves actively listening for the inner promptings of the Holy Spirit. Isaiah says that his ear is wakened each morning so he can listen like one being taught. 'The Sovereign Lord has opened my ears' (Isaiah 50:4, 5). This is a good example of how we are to listen – to open our inner ears as students listening avidly to what their master has in store for them each day. Luke 8:18 records Jesus telling the disciples to 'consider carefully how you listen'. The activity is to assist with this.

Activity

The activity requires three different kinds of sound to listen to (see the note above). Allow the group to make themselves comfortable and prepare to really listen to these three different sections that you will play. Do not tell them what you are going to play, just say they will be listening to different snippets and will then have some time to listen to silence. The whole activity should take about 12–15 minutes.

1. Play the first snippet – for example, the spoken voice, some music or nature sounds. It should last about two to three minutes.
2. Repeat for the other two sounds, leaving some silence between each snippet.
3. Then tell people that there will be another few minutes to listen to the silence.

Allow a couple of minutes for people to assess the activity.

Short discussion

In pairs discuss how you found listening to these different areas. What is it like to 'consider carefully how you listen'?

Bible reading

John 10:1-6 (The Shepherd and his flock):

'I tell you the truth, the man who does not enter the sheep pen by the gate, but climbs in by some other way, is a thief and a robber. The man who enters by the gate is the shepherd of his sheep. The watchman opens the gate for him, and the sheep listen to his voice. He calls his own sheep by name and leads them out. When he has brought out all his own, he goes on ahead of them, and his sheep follow him because they know his voice. But they will never follow a stranger; in fact, they will run away from him because they do not recognise a stranger's voice.' Jesus used this figure of speech, but they did not understand what he was telling them.

Just having the physical space put aside for God is sometimes not enough for us to hear the divine voice within. It is also allowing space in our minds, which can get full of thoughts and worries and into a busy state. When the mind experiences a more relaxed state, there is more clarity to hear and notice what is going on around us. It is also easier for us to tap into pleasure and humour. This means having the mind focus on the here and now, living in the present moment, rather than whirring away about other issues at the same time. It is in this present state that the sheep can recognise that voice of the Shepherd.

Eastern sheepfolds had only one door, which was guarded by a watchman when several flocks were enclosed. The watchman is there as an observer. In Week 1, we looked at using our imaginations to observe with Jesus. This observer position is a good one to oversee our thoughts and whether our minds are in a state to be able to recognise the Shepherd and to hear his voice.

We need to trust that, since we are a sheep of the Shepherd, we have the ability to recognise and hear his voice. We need to work out the best conditions for us to hear that voice. Finding activities like meditation and relaxation exercises that bring the mind into a calm state can help. Recognising the voice is noticing what leads us in the direction of love: love of God, of ourselves and of others. It is hearing the voice that leads to life – to wholeness, to feeling more together, to more energy – to the full life that Jesus offers. Anything that draws us to wisdom, beauty, joy, faith and love will be where God is. We have many conflicting voices within, some that pull our thoughts down the negative path. These will not be the thoughts that turn us towards God; they will pull us away. We need to listen to the difference, which will help us to find God's voice.

Stephen, whom we met earlier, decided to take time out of each day for the period of Advent. He had to get up earlier, but it was something he wanted to do. He tried just sitting quietly and letting his mind relax, trying to brush away any thoughts that came into his head. Sometimes he focused on a Bible verse, sometimes a word, or an image. He did find it hard to be still, but enjoyed just sitting peacefully in God's presence, just allowing himself to be met by God. He found it altered his day and he often ended his day with some quiet, as he felt something profound was happening in this time.

Short discussion

In pairs, discuss the implications in this Bible passage of the sheep hearing the shepherd's voice. Can you hear that voice? Do you notice what blocks or clouds that divine voice? Is there anything you would like to do this Advent to help you listen to God?

Summary

God speaks to us in secrets. We need to consider how we listen so we can uncover his meaning.

Prayer

Spend a few minutes sitting in God's presence. Try to calm any inner chatter. Just open your inner ears and listen for that voice of the Shepherd.

Further activity

This activity uses the imagination with the John 10 passage. Using the imagination does help the mind to get into the relaxed state – a good state in which to hear the voice of the Shepherd. So just get yourself sitting comfortably. Perhaps have your feet flat on the floor.

Read through the following two verses: 'The man who enters by the gate is the shepherd of his sheep. The watchman opens the gate for him, and the sheep listen to his voice. He calls his own sheep by name and leads them out.'

See if you can imagine this scene: there are sheep in a sheep pen with a watchman and a shepherd. Try to see this image in your mind. What are the sounds you can hear? Are there any smells you notice or anything you can feel?

Now, in this scene, put yourself in the place of the watchman. This is the person who is noticing everything. You can see all around you. You notice which sheep you are. Have a look at that sheep. What is it doing? What is it thinking? What is it feeling?

Now you notice the shepherd who is the shepherd for that sheep. Have a good look at the shepherd. What is the shepherd saying to the sheep?

Listen to the shepherd calling your name. Can you allow him to lead you as the sheep out of the sheep pen? Just imagine this scene and what happens next.

Acknowledge what has gone on for you before you bring yourself back from your imagination.

6. Regina Coupar, *The Art of Soul: An Artist's Guide to Spirituality* (Editions Novalis), p. 34.

Week 5

By his wounds we are healed

Introduction

Advent can be a difficult time for people going through suffering. Christmas highlights family ties and social contacts. It is a time for remembering other family Christmases and loved ones. For those who are lonely, bereaved or going through suffering of any kind, this period can be a time of pain and vulnerability. This week we are looking at the difficulty of getting through the Advent period when going through suffering. It may be that you are in this position yourself or you know of others who are. We look to Jesus who suffered for us and who has enabled our healing through his wounds.

Richard Rohr defines suffering simply as 'whenever you are not in control'.[7] So we can suffer in small ways throughout the day and also in ways that affect us greatly, bringing much chaos into our lives. We often want control in our lives and suffering takes us out of our comfort zone.

The circumstances of Jesus' birth were surrounded by chaos: the long journey that Mary and Joseph took to Bethlehem, the sparse nature of their surroundings for the birth and King Herod threatening Jesus' death. One of the gifts the Magi brought for Jesus was myrrh, precious oil used to anoint the dead. It signified the suffering that Jesus would go through in his life and the effect of this on Mary. We will look more to his suffering throughout this week.

God is a God of wholeness and healing. Jesus lived a life of wholeness which was made up of being together with God and man, loving the poor and weak, teaching and healing, but also much suffering. We can read about that suffering in Isaiah 53: the whole chapter graphically portrays the suffering Jesus was to bear. These verses are from Isaiah 53:3-5:

> We despised him and rejected him; he endured suffering and pain. No one would even look at him – we ignored him as if he were nothing. But he endured the suffering that should have been ours, the pain that we should have borne. All the while we thought that his suffering was punishment sent by God. But because of our sins he was wounded, beaten because of the evil we did. We are healed by the punishment he suffered, made whole by the blows he received. (Good News Bible)

Somehow by these wounds that Jesus endured we can be made whole. Suffering is very much part of the whole life that we are offered. Maybe we are more mouldable in these times, so we can be shaped into the person God has planned for us to be. In Psalm 139:15, 16 David says, 'My frame was not hidden from you when I was made in the secret place, when I was woven together in the depths of the earth. Your eyes saw my unformed body; all the days ordained for me were written in your book before one of them came to be.' God knows the person we are made to be with all our unique gifts. Suffering takes us outside our comfort zone, shakes us up, challenges our faith, but somehow God gives us resources through the hard times that seem to aide our purpose in life.

In her book *Hinds' Feet in High Places*[8] Hannah Hurnard tells an allegory about a person called Much Afraid who is taken on a difficult journey to the mountain tops by the Shepherd (representing Jesus). She learns various lessons throughout the hard journey, and for each lesson she collects a pebble. At the end of this journey, Jesus then takes her pebbles and makes them into glorious, sparkling jewels which he sets into a crown for her to wear. This is a good symbol for those going through suffering – holding on to the lessons learnt through the hard times and allowing those hard-earned pebbles to be made into a crown of blessing; a crown that will be significant in the life to come.

This may be a thorny session. We all have our sufferings to bear – some more difficult than others. There will be a need for compassion for each individual on how much they think about their suffering, and also collectively as a group, as each person shares a little of that suffering. So as you prepare to think about how suffering has shaped your life, do it in a loving way, allowing Jesus to come alongside you as you reflect.

Preparation

Think about an incident in your life when you have not been in control. Reflect on whether this had any influence on your faith. Did you experience any connection to God through this incidence?

You may also like to read through Isaiah 53: The Suffering Servant.

Note on the activity

The activity in this session uses plasticine. This can be bought at any shop that sells children's craft activities. Different colours are good to have, and the plasticine is often bought in strips. Two strips should be plenty for each person. It is important that people are reassured that they are not being asked to make anything, just to use their hands to shape and mould. It is the process that is important rather than the end result.

Session 5: By his wounds we are healed

Equipment

Bible, plasticine (children's pack will be fine, having strips of different colours is helpful) and mats or plastic/paper plates on which to mould the plasticine.

Quiet time

Sit silently in God's presence. Allow any tensions to relax and just sit allowing yourself to be loved by God.

Opening prayer

See from his head, his hands, his feet,
sorrow and love flow mingling down.
Did e'er such love and sorrow meet,
or thorns compose so rich a crown?[9]

Lord, be with us now as we contemplate our sufferings in the light of the suffering you endured for us. We pray for your love to meet with our sorrow. Amen.

Commentary

This week we are looking at the difficulties of suffering at this Advent time. Christmas can bring up painful memories, can highlight loneliness and be a time when we cope with more chaos in our lives. In this session we will be looking at how our sufferings may have shaped us and how Jesus' sufferings influence our lives.

This is Jackie's situation:

Hello, I am Jackie. I find Christmas really hard as my mother and father both died in December, two years ago in a car crash. I don't know how I got through Christmas that year. It was taken up with funeral arrangements, form filling and having to tell others about what had happened, with an immobilising grief clouding every move. Since then I have just wanted to hide away at Christmas time. I wish December would just be scrapped every year and I could go from November to January. I have been really struggling with my faith since this happened, but I know that somehow God is giving me the strength to get through the dark times. I do have my husband and two children to consider. The children get so excited and I love their anticipation. I don't want to spoil that but I find it so hard to join in their excitement. This year I am going to try and bring my mum and dad into Christmas time, instead of struggling with my thoughts of them. I might write them a letter and I will go through some photos of them with the children.

In Week 3, we looked at being who we are: a unique person in Christ. We looked at what pressures can do to change our shape. Suffering can affect who we are, can change our shape. It may bring up all sorts of feelings – emotions that we might not have dealt with before. Grief, anger, resentment, helplessness, pain, depression can all be a big influence in trying to find the way through the suffering. We will be thinking about how God ministers to us in these difficult times.

As mentioned in the introduction, suffering can be any time where we are not in control. We are going to explore a time where we have not felt in control and the influence of Jesus in our suffering through the next activity and later Bible passages. The activity is going to be split into two parts.

Activity – Part 1

Place the plasticine in the middle of the group. Encourage everyone to take some. The instructions are to sit reflecting on a time when you have not felt in control in your life. As you ponder, just manipulate the plasticine. Don't think about making something, just use the hands to squeeze and mould. Something might transpire, but the end result is not important. Time 10 minutes.

Just lay down your plasticine for the moment. We are now going to look at Jesus' suffering and then continue with part two of the activity.

Bible readings

Christ suffered for you, leaving you an example, that you should follow in his steps. 'He committed no sin, and no deceit was found in his mouth.' When they hurled their insults at him, he did not retaliate; when he suffered, he made no threats. Instead, he entrusted himself to him who judges justly. He himself bore our sins in his body on the cross, so that we might die to sins and live for righteousness; by his wounds you have been healed. (1 Peter 2:21-24)

For God, who said, 'Let light shine out of darkness,' made his light shine in our hearts to give us the light of the knowledge of God's glory displayed in the face of Christ.

But we have this treasure in jars of clay to show that this all-surpassing power is from God and not from us. We are hard pressed on every side, but not crushed; perplexed, but not in despair; persecuted, but not abandoned; struck down, but not destroyed. We always carry around in our body the death of Jesus, so that the life of Jesus may also be revealed in our body. (2 Corinthians 4:6-10)

These are verses written by Peter and Paul with regard to Jesus' suffering. How did Jesus cope with his last week of suffering? In his last few days on earth he actually became very passive. A lot was done to him: he was flogged by the soldiers, tortured and mocked, and was told to carry his own cross. He let others do things to him. In fact he was too weak to carry such a heavy cross so Simon of Cyrene was roped in to carry it. Sometimes what can help us in difficult times is to allow ourselves to receive, receive from others, but also receive the comfort and love with which God wants to bless us.

Paul describes the effect of Jesus' death on his own suffering. He finds God's secrets through his connection with Jesus and feels his power and light aiding him in his difficulties.

Activity – Part 2

There will be 10 more minutes to reflect on Jesus' suffering. You can return to your plasticine, use more if you wish, letting your hands mould and play with it as you think about the suffering of Jesus. Or you can use this time to reflect on the Bible verses.

Now just acknowledge what has gone on for you and look at what has developed out of the plasticine.

Allow some time to get together in pairs and share how that exercise was. Stress that people do not need to share any personal details.

Bible reading

John 20:19, 20, 26-28 (Jesus appears to his disciples):

> On the evening of that first day of the week, when the disciples were together, with the doors locked for fear of the Jewish leaders, Jesus came and stood among them and said, 'Peace be with you!' After he said this, he showed them his hands and side. The disciples were overjoyed when they saw the Lord.
>
> A week later his disciples were in the house again, and Thomas was with them. Though the doors were locked, Jesus came and stood among them and said, 'Peace be with you!' Then he said to Thomas, 'Put your finger here; see my hands. Reach out your hand and put it into my side. Stop doubting and believe.' Thomas said to him, 'My Lord and my God!'

Jesus was recognised by his wounds; he had to show the disciples his hands and his side for them to recognise him. Henri Nouwen says,

> Jesus is the Lord who came to save us on the cross. The wounds in Jesus' glorified body remind us of the way in which we are saved. But they also remind us that our wounds are much more than road blocks on our way to God. They show us the unique way to follow the suffering Christ, and they are destined to become glorified in our resurrected life. Just as Jesus was identified by his wounds, so are we.[10]

Our wounds can be an opening into following a closer path with Jesus if we allow him, the suffering servant, to lead. Our wounds can shape us into the person God has in mind for us to be.

Jackie, whom we met earlier, still found it painful going through this Advent time. However, bringing memories of her parents into this time, through her prayer times and sharing with her children, did help to make them part of the celebration, instead of separate. She found she shed many tears in her quiet times with God, but they seemed to give her a sense of peace. Jackie also found a counsellor to talk through things and this helped to lift a heavy burden from her. She did find she had more understanding for others going along similar paths.

Short discussion

In pairs, discuss how the suffering of Jesus might affect the way we cope with times when we are not in control. Do you think the difficult times in your life have shaped you and shown your uniqueness?

Summary

In this session we have explored a creative way of looking at our suffering and have looked to Jesus and his suffering to help explore these difficult times. This may have been a difficult session for many. You may need to look after yourself in the time after the session.

Prayer

Spend some time reflecting on the session. Reflect with your plasticine and bring it to God. Talk with him about what has gone on for you. Listen to his answers.

Circle me prayer

Circle me, O God, keep peace within and anxiety out.
Circle me, O God, keep love within and hatred out.
Circle me, O God, keep light within and darkness out.

Further activity

Read through 2 Corinthians 1:3-7 (Paul gives thanks to God):

Let us give thanks to the God and Father of our Lord Jesus Christ, the merciful Father, the God from whom all help comes! He helps us in all our troubles, so that we are able to help others who have all kinds of troubles, using the same help that we ourselves have received from God. Just as we have a share in Christ's many sufferings, so also through Christ we share in God's great help. If we suffer, it is for your help and salvation; if we are helped, then you too are helped and given the strength to endure with patience the same sufferings that we also endure. So our hope in you is never shaken; we know that just as you share in our sufferings, you also share in the help we receive. (Good News Bible.)

Paul was able to use the comfort that he found through God in his sufferings to be able to comfort others. There are always people who need comfort and help in their sufferings. Each of us will have our own difficulties that we have managed in different ways. Use the Bible passage to reflect on how your difficulties might be used to help others. Is there someone you could help out at this Advent time?

7. Richard Rohr, *Things Hidden: Scripture as Spirituality* (Saint Anthony Messenger Press), p. 191.
8. Hannah Hurnard, *Hinds' Feet in High Places* (Kingsway Publications).
9. Isaac Watts, *When I survey the wondrous cross*, verse 3.
10. Henri Nouwen, *Jesus: A Gospel* (Orbis Books), p. 113.

Week 6

I bring you good news of great joy

Introduction

This week we will be celebrating Jesus coming to earth as a human and the joy that he offers us in our lives now. We think about the effect that God's joy can make in the worries and fears in this life. There will be a chance to reflect on the course so far and what God might be drawing you to.

Over the last few weeks we have looked at issues that affect us, especially at Advent time. It is easy to allow the mind to worry and fret over many concerns. Sometimes what starts off as a small doubt or something trivial can set the mind into a negative cycle that can draw in other anxieties and fears, not leaving any room to connect to joy. In Week 4 we looked at being a watchman to our thoughts and noting when they stop us being able to open that inner ear. Being this observer of our mind helps us to see whether anxieties or fears are a barrier to the joy that Jesus is offering.

Jesus offers us his joy that comes from God as its source, so it endures through all circumstances. Jesus speaks of it in John 15:9-11: 'As the Father has loved me, so have I loved you. Now remain in my love. If you keep my commands, you will remain in my love, just as I have kept my Father's commands and remain in his love. I have told you this so that my joy may be in you and that your joy may be complete.' C. S. Lewis called joy an 'unsatisfied desire which is itself more desirable than any other satisfaction'.[11] He said that it must be distinguished from both happiness and pleasure, which are more transient. Jesus says in John 16:22 that no one can take away this joy: it is always there if we are connected to God.

Any interaction with Jesus is an opportunity to connect to this joy. Mary found this connection early on in her vocation as the mother of Jesus. She must have been really worried about her pregnancy and her circumstances. She took herself off to stay with her cousin Elizabeth whom the angel had told her was also pregnant. The reaction of Elizabeth to her greeting must have been one that reassured her and gave her joy. We read of this in Luke 1:41-45:

> When Elizabeth heard Mary's greeting, the baby leaped in her womb, and Elizabeth was filled with the Holy Spirit. In a loud voice she exclaimed: 'Blessed are you among women, and blessed is the child you will bear! But why am I so favoured, that the mother of my Lord should come to me? As soon as the sound of your greeting reached my ears, the baby in my womb leaped for joy. Blessed is she who has believed that what the Lord has said to her will be accomplished!'

The joy that Jesus offers can even be felt by a foetus in a womb. This must have been such a reassuring sign to Mary that somehow Elizabeth *knew* the Lord before she had even spoken of it. God has a way of getting through to us his joy and reassurance in difficult times.

G. K. Chesterton wrote that joy is the gigantic secret of the Christian. He said that Jesus showed his tears and anger but always restrained something. 'There was some one thing that was too great for God to show us when he walked upon our earth; and I have sometimes fancied that it was his mirth.'[12] God *knows* that all will be well. He has to listen to our fears and worries but he knows the outcome. The joy of the Lord is made complete when we come to the day when we finally see face-to-face that for which we were made.

Preparation

Take some time to review the last few weeks that you have been doing this course and note what God has been showing you or leading you to. Is there anything you have done that has drawn you nearer God? Is there anything you have done where you haven't felt so close to God?

Think of a symbol of what Jesus means to you. It could be an image you have or an object. If possible bring it along to the session – either physically or in your imagination.

Session 6: I bring you good news of great joy

Equipment

Bible, paper and pens, celebration cake.

Quiet time

In the quiet, sit with God and let your memory wander to a time when you had a really good laugh or when you were filled with joy. Try to re-experience those feelings. Allow laughter to erupt – it can be catching!

Opening prayer

'The hopes and fears of all the years are met in thee tonight.' Thank you, Lord, that through you our hopes and our fears can be transformed. Be with us now as we explore the joy that you want to offer us, joy that will overcome all fears. Amen.

Commentary

The last few weeks we have been exploring different aspects of ourselves and how Jesus speaks into those issues. This week we look at the joy that Jesus brings to us: a joy that can be experienced through all our worries and fears.

Short discussion

In pairs, spend a few minutes sharing about the course and what has gone on for you over the last few weeks. Are there any aspects that have brought you closer to God?

In Week 4 we looked at the best state for our minds to hear the voice of God. Focusing on the here and now and using calming activities can be helpful. Our minds are often conditioned to be in a state of high arousal as we flit from one job to the next, often using technology for long periods of time. Fear and anxiety can fuel this state and can become barriers to the joy that is ours from God.

Jesus offers us his joy that comes from God as its source, so it endures through all circumstances. In the Gospel of John, Jesus speaks of this gift: 'These things I have spoken to you, that my joy may remain in you, and that your joy may be full' (John 15:11, NKJV). Sometimes we cannot connect to this joy as we feel we don't deserve it, or think it wouldn't be right under certain circumstances, for instance, if we are suffering. But we have this God-given gift to celebrate and enjoy. Christ came and declared a wedding feast, a celebration, at the very centre of life. In Psalm 23 David points out that God prepares a feast 'in the presence of my enemies'. God does not want us to wait for the right time to connect to this joy; he offers it through all that we experience.

The following activity is a meditation taking something that we fear, then connecting to the joy that Jesus offers.

Activity

This activity is a meditation on Luke 2:8-16 – the shepherds hearing about the Messiah. Reassure people that it does not matter if they follow their own thread through this time. It is in four parts and if people find they want to stop at one part and not follow all the way through then that is fine. The meditation needs to be read out slowly. Allow a few minutes between each part (three to four minutes with a couple of extra minutes at the end). The whole meditation should take between 15 and 20 minutes. Allow people to get themselves in a comfortable position, and to prepare to use their imaginations. Read out the whole passage to start:

The Shepherds and the Angels

And there were shepherds living out in the fields nearby, keeping watch over their flocks at night. An angel of the Lord appeared to them, and the glory of the Lord shone around them, and they were terrified. But the angel said to them, 'Do not be afraid. I bring you good news of great joy that will be for all the people. Today in the town of David a Saviour has been born to you; he is Christ the Lord. This will be a sign to you: You will find a baby wrapped in cloths and lying in a manger.'

Suddenly a great company of the heavenly host appeared with the angel, praising God and saying,

'Glory to God in the highest, and on earth peace to all on whom his favour rests.'

When the angels had left them and gone into heaven, the shepherds said to one another, 'Let's go to Bethlehem and see this thing that has happened, which the Lord has told us about.'

So they hurried off and found Mary and Joseph, and the baby, who was lying in the manger.

Part 1. Imagine yourself in a field. Just let a scene emerge as you sit in the quiet.

You reflect on one thing that is agitating you at the moment, something that is making you anxious or fearful. Just observe those feelings. Perhaps they might resonate somewhere in your body.

Part 2. An angel appears to you in your field. The angel tells you not to be afraid. Hear those words. He has a message for you: 'I bring you good news of great joy.' Listen to the message the angel has just for you.

Part 3. Now a whole host of angels is in your field, telling you of the great joy that has come into the world. Hear their joy; imagine what happens.

Part 4. You get led to see the baby Jesus. Spend some time with Jesus. You might like to imagine bringing a symbol to him, something that connects you to him. See what happens in the scene.

Just acknowledge what has gone on for you in the meditation.

When you are ready slowly bring yourselves back into the room.

Split into pairs for people to share how that was for them. Stress that people do not have to share anything personal.

Jesus comes so that we can experience life to the full, including the joy that is ours – a gift from God. Sometimes we find it hard to feel this joy but it will be there. Jesus says in John 16:22 that no one can take away this joy – it is always there if we are connected to God: 'Therefore you now have sorrow; but I will see you again and your heart will rejoice, and your joy no one will take from you' (NKJV).

We need to take away obstacles that might be preventing us from connecting to that joy within us and learn to celebrate with Jesus.

Have a time of sharing your symbols that represent Jesus. Let them lead into a prayer time.

Then share the celebratory cake and enjoy fellowship together.

Further activity

I think Jesus' ideal Christmas celebration could be something like the one that is found in John 12:1-3 (Jesus anointed at Bethany):

Six days before the Passover, Jesus arrived at Bethany, where Lazarus lived, whom Jesus had raised from the dead. Here a dinner was given in Jesus' honour. Martha served, while Lazarus was among those reclining at the table with him. Then Mary took about a pint of pure nard, an expensive perfume; she poured it on Jesus' feet and wiped his feet with her hair. And the house was filled with the fragrance of the perfume.

Jesus had raised Lazarus from the dead and was now celebrating with him and his friends. Imagine that celebration – someone who was dead being brought back to life. This was a meal in Jesus' honour. I expect Martha had pulled out all the stops and produced a lovely spread. Mary really wanted to acknowledge her love of Jesus and this was how she worshipped him. Just be with them in this celebration. Imagine the scene, the joy that must have been there, the good food and fellowship. Use your senses to really get into the picture. Then see how you would like to worship Jesus. What would you like to bring to him? Just take some time to worship Jesus and experience his love and joy.

11. C. S. Lewis, *Surprised by Joy* (HarperCollins), pp. 17–18.
12. G. K. Chesterton, *Orthodoxy* (Bantam Doubleday Dell), pp. 166–7.